Instant Pot
ELEVATED

Flo Lum

PHOTOGRAPHS BY DUDE

For Dude

Contents

Introduction

Many appliances come and go in my kitchen but after four years of using the Instant Pot, it is still the most used kitchen appliance. In this recipe collection, you will find more Asian recipes, as I have been making a lot of childhood favourites to introduce to my kids, in hopes that they will also be some of their childhood favourites.

My recipes are simple, using ordinary ingredients that your whole family will enjoy. However, I often use techniques that will elevate the flavours, going beyond a "dump and go" type of recipe. They are never fussy or complicated.

The recipes in this cookbook should work with other electric pressure cookers with similar features to the Instant Pot. If your electric pressure cooker does not have a sauté/browning function, you can sauté on the stovetop and transfer the ingredients to your pressure cooker. All the recipes are written to work optimally in a 6 quart pressure cooker.

With over 88,000 subscribers on my YouTube channel and with some urging from my audience, I was encouraged to write a second recipe book. Thank you for letting me share a little bit of my simple, ordinary and joyful life and for welcoming me, through my recipes, into your home.

From Your Kitchen

I always love hearing from YouTube viewers that have tried and enjoyed my recipes. With this cookbook, show me how these recipes work out for you and your family. Make sure to tag #flolumcookbook and @flolum in your posts and stories on Instagram, Facebook and Twitter!

Sides

Creamy Dill Potato Salad
Egg Salad
Pearl Couscous with Spinach
Hummus
White Bean Dip

Creamy Dill Potato Salad

This is not your typical potato salad with egg and mayo. Instead, I make it with a creamy dill dressing and add some bacon. I brought this to a summer potluck and everyone loved it.

Makes 6-8 servings

2 pounds white or red skinned baby potatoes, halved
1 tablespoon kosher salt
¼ cup mayonnaise
2 tablespoons plain yogurt
1 tablespoon apple cider vinegar
1 teaspoon dijon mustard
1½ teaspoon dried dill
¼ teaspoon kosher salt
¼ teaspoon freshly ground black pepper
½ small shallot, finely diced
1 green onion, chopped
4 slices bacon, cooked and crumbled
kosher salt
freshly ground black pepper

If not using baby potatoes, cut white or red potatoes into 1½ inch pieces.

---

1. Place a trivet in the inner cooking pot and add 1 cup water. Add potatoes and season with salt.

2. Close and lock the lid, making sure the steam knob is on Sealing/Locked. Pressure cook on high for 5 minutes.

3. Meanwhile, prepare the dressing. In a large mixing bowl, mix the mayonnaise, yogurt, vinegar, mustard, dill, salt and pepper. Refrigerate until ready to use.

4. Once the pressure cooking is done, quick release the pressure. Drain the potatoes and let cool.

5. Add potatoes, shallot, green onion and bacon to the dressing, toss well. Season with salt and pepper to taste.

Egg Salad

I absolutely hate peeling eggs, so this method helps me to make egg salad more often. I prefer my egg salad plain and basic. You can add mustard, sweet pickles, dill or whatever else to make your favourite egg salad.

Makes 4 servings

6 eggs
1 green onion, chopped
¼ cup mayonnaise
kosher salt
freshly ground black pepper

1. Break the eggs into an oven safe bowl.

2. Place a trivet in the inner cooking pot and add 1 cup of water. Place the bowl on top of the trivet and cover with a silicone lid or aluminum foil.

3. Close and lock the lid, making sure the steam knob is on Sealing/Locked. Pressure cook on high for 5 minutes.

4. Once the pressure cooking is done, quick release the pressure.

5. Chop up the egg loaf.

6. Stir in remaining ingredients. Season with salt and pepper to taste, mix well.

Pearl Couscous with Spinach

We eat a lot of rice, so this is a tasty elevated side alternative to serve with a meat entrée. It's also a deliciously easy way to incorporate a vegetable into you meal.

Makes 4 servings

1 tablespoon butter
1 tablespoon olive oil
1 small onion, sliced
2 cloves garlic, minced
1 cup pearl or Israeli couscous
2 cups chicken broth
6 oz spinach
kosher salt
freshly ground black pepper

---

1. Press Sauté, adjust it to high heat. Once the pot is hot, heat olive oil and melt butter. Add onion and sauté for 3 minutes. Add garlic, cook for another 30 seconds until fragrant.

2. Add couscous and cook for 1-2 minutes until toasted. Season with salt and pepper. Cancel Sauté.

3. Add chicken broth, making sure all the couscous is submerged.

4. Close and lock the lid, making sure the steam knob is on Sealing/Locked. Pressure cook on high for 5 minutes

5. Once the pressure cooking is done, quick release the pressure.

6. Stir in spinach until wilted. Season with salt and pepper to taste.

Hummus

This Middle Eastern dip is great as a side dish or on its own. Forget about getting it from the deli, make it easily at home. Great with pita, baguette or veggie sticks. I especially enjoy eating hummus with grilled or roasted vegetables.

Makes 2 cups

BEANS
¾ cup dried chickpeas
4 cups water
1 tablespoon olive oil
¼ teaspoon salt
3 cloves garlic, bruised

DIP
2 tablespoons lemon juice
½ cup tahini
1 teaspoon kosher salt
2 tablespoons extra virgin olive oil, plus more for serving
pinch paprika

---

1. Rinse beans. In the inner cooking pot, add beans, water, olive oil, salt, and garlic.

2. Close and lock the lid, making sure the steam knob is on Sealing/Locked. Pressure cook on high for 35 minutes.

3. Once the pressure cooking is done, quick release the pressure.

4. Drain beans, save 1 cup of liquid.

5. In a food processor, combine tahini and lemon juice and process for 1 minute. Scrape down the sides.

6. Add cooked chickpeas and garlic, salt and ½ cup chickpea water. Blend for a minute or two until smooth. Add more chickpea liquid if you want a thinner hummus. Scrape down the sides.

7. While processor is on, slowly pour in olive oil.

8. Place hummus in a bowl. The longer it sits, the more the flavors blend. Serve with a drizzle of extra virgin olive oil on top and a pinch of paprika. Enjoy warm or at room temperature with pita bread and veggie sticks.

If a stronger garlic flavour is desired, add 1-2 cloves garlic when blending.

White Bean Dip

I needed another dip for my husband's 50th birthday 'Grazing Table' and made this dip. It's easy to make and delivers a wonderful smooth lemony flavour.

Makes 2 cups

BEANS
¾ cup dried cannellini beans
4 cups water
1 tablespoon olive oil
¼ teaspoon kosher salt
1 clove garlic, bruised
1 bay leaf

DIP
1-2 cloves garlic
zest from 1 lemon
1 tablespoon freshly squeezed lemon juice
¼ cup extra virgin olive oil
½ teaspoon kosher salt
¼ teaspoon freshly ground black pepper

———————

1. Rinse beans. In the inner cooking pot, add beans, water, olive oil, salt, garlic and bay leaf.

2. Close and lock the lid, making sure the steam knob is on Sealing/Locked. Pressure cook on high for 35 minutes.

3. Once the pressure cooking is done, quick release the pressure. Drain beans. Remove bay leaf and garlic.

4. In a food processor, combine beans, 1-2 cloves garlic, lemon zest and lemon juice. Pulse a few times to get the mixture going. While processor is on, slowly pour in olive oil. Season with salt and pepper and pulse until mixed well.

5. Pour into a small bowl. Serve with pita bread and vegetable sticks.

Soups & Stews

Beef Barley

Vietnamese Beef Noodle Soup (Pho Bo)

Irish Stew

Hong Kong Borscht

Mom's Beef Stew

Chicken Congee

Malaysian Chicken Laksa

Creamy Chicken and Rice Soup

Chicken Tortilla Soup

Egg Drop Soup with Chicken

Chicken Cacciatore

White Turkey Chili

Fish Chowder

Malaysian Seafood Laksa

Creamy Seafood Chowder

Hot and Sour Soup

Miso Ramen Faster

Sausage, Kale and Couscous Soup

Pork Belly and Sausage Cassoulet

Pork Chile Verde

French Onion Soup

Leek and Potato Soup

Roasted Tomato Soup

Cheesy Broccoli Soup

Corn and Potato Chowder

Cream of Mushroom

Beef Barley Soup

This is the only way I eat barley. It makes this soup so much more hearty. This soup is filled with beef and veggies and is perfect to warm your tummy on a chilly day.

Makes 4-6 servings

1 pound stewing beef, 1 inch pieces
1 teaspoon kosher salt
¼ teaspoon freshly ground black pepper
2 tablespoons olive oil
1 onion, 1 inch pieces
2 stalks celery, 1 inch pieces
4 carrots, 1 inch pieces
2 cloves garlic, minced
½ cup dried pearl barley, rinsed

1 teaspoon dried thyme
2 teaspoons dried parsley
1 bay leaf
1 tablespoon tomato paste
6 cups beef broth
1 teaspoon kosher salt
½ teaspoon freshly ground black pepper
¼ cup Italian parsley, chopped

1. Season beef with 1 teaspoon kosher salt and ¼ teaspoon pepper.

2. Press Sauté, adjust it to high heat. Once the pot is hot, heat olive oil. In small batches, brown the meat on each side without overcrowding. Remove the meat and place in a bowl.

3. Add more olive oil to the pot, if needed. Add onion, celery, and carrots and sauté for 3 minutes. Season with 1 teaspoon salt and ¼ teaspoon pepper. Add garlic, cook for another 30 seconds until fragrant. Add barley and cook it for another minute.

4. Pour in 1 cup broth to deglaze, scraping up any brown bits from the bottom of the pot. Cancel Sauté.

5. Add the beef with the juices, thyme, parsley, bay leaf, tomato paste, remaining beef broth. Close and lock the lid, making sure the steam knob is on Sealing/Locked. Pressure cook on high for 20 minutes.

6. Once the pressure cooking is done, quick or natural release the pressure.

7. Remove bay leaf. Stir in chopped parsley.

8. Serve in individual bowls with crusty bread.

Vietnamese Beef Noodle Soup (Pho Bo)

For our family, this satisfying soup noodle is a staple dish that hits the spot on rainy, chilly days. We often get takeout Pho but will be making this at home more often. Bonus points for not having to go out in the rain!

Makes 4-6 servings

1½ pound beef bones
2½ pounds beef shin
1 pound beef brisket
1 tablespoon oil
2 onions halved
3 oz ginger (4 inch knob), sliced
2 star anise
1 tablespoon rock sugar
4 whole cloves
½ teaspoon ground coriander (or 1 teaspoon whole coriander)
1 cinnamon stick
¼ cup fish sauce
1 teaspoon kosher salt
8 cups water

TO SERVE
1-1½ pound rice stick noodles, cooked following package instructions
4-6 green onion, chopped
½-¾ bunch cilantro, chopped
½-¾ pound bean sprouts
4-6 stems Thai basil
4-6 Thai chili peppers, sliced
1 lime cut into 8 wedges
hoisin sauce
Sriracha sauce

---

1. Rinse the beef bones and soak them in cold water for about an hour to remove excess blood and impurities. Bring a large pot of water to boil. Give the bones another rinse then add them to the boiling water along with the beef shin and brisket and boil them for 10 minutes. This method is called parboiling which will release more impurities and giving a clearer broth. Drain and rinse the bones and meat under cold water.

2. Press Sauté, adjust it to high heat. Once the pot is hot, heat oil. Add onion and ginger, and char both sides until blackened. This will take about 10 minutes. Cancel Sauté.

3. Add the meat, bones, star anise, rock sugar, cloves, coriander, cinnamon, fish sauce and salt. Add enough water to just cover the ingredients.

4. Close and lock the lid, making sure the steam knob is on Sealing/Locked. Pressure cook on high for 60 minutes.

5. Once the pressure cooking is done, natural pressure release for at least 15 minutes and then quick release the remaining pressure.

6. Remove the brisket and place in the fridge for about 20 minutes before slicing into thin slices. Also, adjust flavour of the soup with more fish sauce and/or salt. In the meantime, prepare the remaining ingredients.

7. Assemble each individual bowl with noodles topped with beef, green onion, cilantro, and bean sprouts. Pour in hot soup and serve with Thai basil, chili peppers, lime, hoisin sauce and Sriracha sauce.

Irish Stew

I recently had the most delicious Irish stew at an Irish pub because where else would I get an amazing bowl of Irish stew? I was not disappointed! It was served with a baguette and no potatoes in the stew. Definitely my kind of stew as I prefer eating it with mashed potatoes on the side instead of potatoes cooked in it. So, of course I had to try to recreate it at home.

Makes 6 servings

1 cup flour
1 tablespoon kosher salt
1 teaspoon freshly ground black pepper
3 pounds boneless beef short-rib, 1½ inch pieces
2 tablespoons butter
2 tablespoons olive oil
2 large onion, cut into eighths
6 carrots, 2 inch pieces
4 cloves garlic, minced
1 cup Guinness beer
1 tablespoon tomato paste
1 tablespoon worcestershire sauce
2 teaspoons dried thyme
2 bay leaves
2 teaspoon salt
½ teaspoon freshly ground black pepper
1 tablespoon Italian parsley, chopped

———

1. In a bowl, combine flour, salt and pepper. Add beef pieces and lightly coat.

2. Press Sauté, adjust it to high heat. Once the pot is hot, heat olive oil and melt butter. In small batches, brown the meat on each side without overcrowding. Remove the meat and place in a bowl.

3. Add more olive oil to the pot, if needed. Add carrots and onions and sauté for 3 minutes. Add garlic, cook for another 30 seconds until fragrant.

4. Pour in the Guinness to deglaze, scraping up any brown bits from the bottom of the pot. Cook for 2 minutes. Cancel Sauté.

5. Return the meat and drippings to the pot. Add the tomato paste, worcestershire sauce, thyme, bay leaves, salt and pepper.

6. Close and lock the lid, making sure the steam knob is on Sealing/Locked. Pressure cook on high for 30 minutes.

7. Once the pressure cooking is done, quick or natural release the pressure.

8. Remove bay leaves. Press Sauté, adjust it to high heat. Cook for another 5 minutes until the sauce thickens.

9. Garnish with chopped parsley. Serve with crusty bread, rice or mashed potatoes.

Hong Kong Borscht

Hong Kong Borscht is not the same as Russian Borscht but delicious nonetheless. This is often offered as part of a set meal at Hong Kong style cafés. Although it does not contain beetroot or sour cream, it is full of vegetables and is sure to fill you up!

Makes 4-6 servings

1 pound beef chuck, cut into 1 inch pieces
1½ teaspoon kosher salt
1 tablespoon vegetable oil
1 oz ginger (2 inch knob), sliced
1 small onion, cut into eighths
1 stalk celery, 1 inch pieces
2 carrots, 1 inch pieces
4-5 cups water
2 cloves garlic, minced

1 bay leaves
1 teaspoon kosher salt
1 teaspoon paprika
½ teaspoon freshly ground black pepper
¼ cup tomato paste
2 tomatoes, chopped
2 white or red potatoes peeled and cut into eighths
¼ cabbage, chopped

1. Season meat with salt.

2. Press Sauté, adjust it to high. Once the pot is hot, heat oil. Add ginger and cook for a minute. In small batches, brown the meat on each side without overcrowding. Remove the meat and place in a bowl.

3. Add onion, celery, and carrots and sauté for 3 minutes. Add garlic, cook for another 30 seconds until fragrant. Pour in 1 cup of water to deglaze, scraping up any brown bits from the bottom of the pot. Cancel Sauté.

4. Add the beef and all the juices back into the pot. Add enough water to just cover the ingredients then place the cabbage on top. Do not stir.

5. Close and lock the lid, making sure the steam knob is on Sealing/Locked. Pressure cook on high for 30 minutes.

6. Once the pressure cooking is done, natural pressure release for at least 15 minutes and then quick release the remaining pressure.

7. Serve in individual bowls with a buttered dinner roll.

Mom's Beef Stew

When I think stew, I think of the savoury meat and potatoes version with the thick dark brown gravy. My mom's version is more like a soup but she called it stew. The broth is light and flavourful and we often eat it with a scoop of rice.

Makes 4-6 servings

1 medium onion, cut into eighths
2 large potatoes, 1½ inch pieces
2 stalks celery, 1½ inch pieces
3 large carrots, 1½ inch pieces
2 oz ginger (3 inch knob), thinly sliced
2 pounds boneless beef short-rib
2 teaspoons salt
freshly ground pepper
6 cups water

———

1. In the inner cooking pot, add onion, potatoes, celery, carrots and ginger.

2. Season beef with salt and pepper. Add beef to the top of the vegetables.

3. Add enough water to just cover the ingredients.

4. Close and lock the lid, making sure the steam knob is on Sealing/Locked. Pressure cook on high for 35 minutes.

5. Once the pressure cooking is done, natural pressure release for at least 15 minutes and then quick release the remaining pressure.

6. Serve in individual bowls with fresh bread or Jasmine rice.

Chicken Congee

Congee is definitely my go-to comfort food for when I am sick or under the weather. There is nothing like a hot bowl of rice porridge to make me feel better.

Makes 4-6 servings

1¼ cups rice
½ teaspoon kosher salt
1 oz ginger (2 inch knob), peeled and thinly sliced
6 chicken thighs
8 cups water
2 teaspoons kosher salt

TO SERVE
soy sauce
sesame oil
ground white pepper
chopped green onions
chopped cilantro
roasted salted peanuts
Chinese donuts, sliced

1. Rinse the rice in a sieve until the water is clear and put it in a small mixing bowl. Stir in ½ teaspoon salt and let marinate for 20-30 minutes.

2. In the inner cooking pot, add chicken, ginger, rice and 2 teaspoons salt. Fill with enough water to reach the 10 cup mark, approximately 8 cups.

3. Close and lock the lid, making sure the steam knob is on Sealing/Locked. Pressure cook on low for 20 minutes.

4. Once the pressure cooking is done, natural pressure release for at least 15 minutes and then quick release the remaining pressure.

5. Remove the chicken. Discard skin and bones and shred the meat. Return the meat to the congee and stir.

6. Serve in individual bowls with a drizzle of soy sauce and sesame oil, a pinch white pepper, green onions, cilantro and peanuts to taste and a side of Chinese donuts.

Malaysian Chicken Laksa

I had never tried laksa until I met Dude. The intense flavours are sure to wow your palette if you have never had it. I used to make the paste from scratch but some of the ingredients are not easily found. Since Dude's mom started buying the paste instead, we did too. By using a paste to simplify the recipe, we definitely make it more often.

Makes 4 servings

1 Basic Asian Chicken Recipe (page 87)
6 cups chicken broth or water
1 package Teans Gourmet Laksa Paste
1 can coconut milk
2 stalks lemongrass, bruised
1 package fried tofu pockets, cut in half
½ pound bean sprouts, blanched
1 cucumber, julienne
4 eggs, medium boiled, cut in half
1 pound thin vermicelli rice noodles, cooked following package instructions

———

1. Make Basic Asian Chicken recipe.

2. Press Sauté. In the same inner cooking pot after making the chicken, add reserved chicken broth and more chicken broth or water to make 6 cups total. Heat until simmering, add paste and stir until paste is dissolved completely. Cancel Sauté. Add coconut milk and lemongrass.

3. Close and lock the lid, making sure the steam knob is on Sealing/Locked. Pressure cook on high for 5 minutes.

4. Once the pressure cooking is done, quick or natural release the pressure.

5. Press Sauté. Add the tofu pockets and heat through.

6. Assemble each individual bowl with noodles topped with bean sprouts, cucumber, egg, and chicken. Pour soup over top.

Creamy Chicken and Rice Soup

This is like the melding of two cultures to me. Having been born and raised in Canada, I know chicken soup is a huge comfort food for many people but congee has always been my source of comfort. So rice in a creamy chicken soup, as no surprise, is doubly comforting.

Makes 4-6 servings

4 chicken thighs
1 teaspoon kosher salt
¼ teaspoon freshly ground black pepper
1 tablespoon olive oil
2 tablespoons butter
3 small carrots, diced
1 medium onion, diced
2 stalks celery, diced
¼ cup flour
4 cups broth
½ teaspoon dried thyme
½ cup long grain rice
1 teaspoon kosher salt
½ teaspoon freshly ground black pepper
1 cup whipping cream
1 tablespoon fresh chopped Italian parsley (garnish)

---

1. Season chicken thighs on both sides with 1 teaspoon kosher salt and ¼ teaspoon pepper.

2. Press Sauté, adjust it to high heat. Once the pot is hot, heat oil. Add chicken, skin side down. Brown for 3 minutes on each side. Remove chicken and set aside.

3. Melt butter, add carrots, onion, and celery to pot and sauté for 3 minutes. Add flour, cook for another minute.

4. Add 1 cup broth to deglaze, scraping up any brown bits from the bottom of the pot. Cancel Sauté.

5. Cover with remaining broth. Add thyme, chicken thighs and any juices, salt and pepper and rice making sure each grain is submerged but do not stir.

6. Close and lock the lid, making sure the steam knob is on Sealing/Locked. Pressure cook on high for 10 minutes.

7. Once the pressure cooking is done, quick or natural release the pressure.

8. Remove chicken, shred meat from skin and bone, and stir shredded meat into the soup.

9. Press Sauté, adjust it to low heat. When the soup begins to simmer, add whipping cream until heated through.

10. Serve in individual bowls. Garnish with extra parsley.

Chicken Tortilla Soup

Having spent a good chunk of time living in California, I miss Mexican flavours a lot. Chicken tortilla soup is one of my favourite soups. It's incredibly comforting and I love the blend of flavours. Hope you enjoy my version of it.

Makes 6-8 servings

8 chicken thighs, boneless, skinless
2 teaspoons kosher salt
1 tablespoon olive oil
1 onion, chopped
6 cloves garlic, minced
2-3 chipotle peppers, chopped
2 (14 oz) cans fire roasted diced tomatoes
1 (4 oz) can chopped mild green chilis
6 cups chicken broth
1 tablespoon chili powder
2 teaspoons dried oregano

½ bunch fresh cilantro, chopped (saving 1 tablespoon for garnish)
3 cups frozen corn, divided
1 cup whipping cream
1 teaspoons kosher salt
1 cup Monterey Jack cheese, shredded
1 avocado, sliced
¼ cilantro, chopped
tortilla chips
lime wedges

1. Season chicken on both sides with kosher salt.

2. Press Sauté, adjust it to high heat. Once the pot is hot, heat oil. In small batches, brown the chicken thighs on each side without overcrowding, about 3 minutes per side. Remove the chicken and place in a bowl.

3. Add onion and sauté for 3 minutes. Add garlic, cook for another 30 seconds until fragrant.

4. Pour in 1 cup broth to deglaze, scraping up any brown bits from the bottom of the pot. Cancel Sauté.

5. Stir in chipotle peppers, tomatoes, chile peppers, remaining broth, chili powder, oregano, cilantro and 2 cups frozen corn.

6. Close and lock the lid, making sure the steam knob is on Sealing/Locked. Pressure cook on high for 10 minutes.

7. Meanwhile, cut the chicken thighs into small bite sized pieces.

8. Once the pressure cooking is done, natural pressure release for at least 15 minutes and then quick release the remaining pressure.

9. Using an immersion blender, blend until smooth.

10. Press Sauté. Stir in remaining 1 cup frozen corn, chicken, whipping cream, 2 teaspoons salt. Heat through.

11. Serve the soup in individual bowls and garnish with cheese, avocado, cilantro, tortilla chips and lime wedge.

Egg Drop Soup with Chicken

I used to make egg drop soup a lot when I was away at university because it was so easy to make. There are many versions out there. This is my version made with corn and chicken and is definitely a step up from my college days.

Makes 4-6 servings

4 chicken thighs
3-4 green onions, cut in half
1 oz ginger (2 inch knob), peeled and thinly sliced
2 cloves garlic, bruised
1½ teaspoon kosher salt
3 cups water
1 14.75 oz can cream style corn
2 teaspoons soy sauce
1 cup frozen corn
2 eggs, lightly beaten
1 green onion, chopped
1 tablespoon cilantro, chopped
ground white pepper

———————

1. In the inner cooking pot and add chicken, green onion, ginger, garlic, salt and water.

2. Close and lock the lid, making sure the steam knob is on Sealing/Locked. Pressure cook on high for 20 minutes.

3. Once the pressure cooking is done, quick or natural release the pressure.

4. Remove the chicken. Discard skin and bones and shred the meat. Set aside.

5. Discard the remaining ingredients and skim off the fat from the broth.

6. Press Sauté. Add cream style corn, soy sauce and frozen corn. Bring it to a simmer. Add the chicken and heat through.

7. While gently stirring the soup, slowly drizzle in the eggs to create the egg ribbons. Cancel Sauté.

8. Stir in green onion and cilantro.

9. Serve in individual bowls with a pinch ground white pepper.

Chicken Cacciatore

My stovetop chicken cacciatore recipe used to take hours but I've adjusted it for the Instant Pot and now it can be done so much faster. A chicken stew is perfectly suited for the cooler, wet weather we get in Vancouver.

Makes 6-8 servings

8 chicken thighs
2 teaspoons kosher salt
½ teaspoon freshly ground black pepper
2 tablespoons olive oil
1 onion, sliced
½ pound white button mushrooms, quartered
1 small orange pepper, sliced
1 small yellow pepper, sliced
2 cloves garlic, minced
2 teaspoons dried thyme

2 teaspoons dried parsley
2 tablespoons tomato paste
1 28 ounce can whole tomatoes
1 tablespoon fresh Italian parsley, chopped

To thicken sauce, press Sauté, adjust it to high heat. Simmer for another 10 minutes until the sauce thickens. Or add a cornstarch slurry:

1. Season chicken with salt and pepper.

2. Press Sauté, adjust it to high heat. Once the pot is hot, heat oil. In small batches, brown the chicken thighs on each side without overcrowding, about 3 minutes per side. Remove the chicken and place in a bowl.

3. Add mushrooms and let brown for a few minutes. Don't stir to get good browning on one side.

4. Stir in the onions. Let cook for a few minutes and scrape up the brown bits from the bottom of the pot. Add peppers and garlic and cook for another minute. Cancel Sauté.

5. Stir in tomato paste. Then add meat with their juices, tomatoes, thyme, and parsley.

6. Close and lock the lid, making sure the steam knob is on Sealing/Locked. Pressure cook on high for 8 minutes.

7. Once the cooking is done, quick release the pressure.

8. Serve with egg noodles or rice.

White Turkey Chili

Makes 6-8 servings

2 tablespoons vegetable oil
1 medium onion, chopped
2 cloves garlic, minced
1 pound ground turkey
1 teaspoon dried oregano
1 teaspoon ground cumin
1 teaspoon cayenne pepper (optional)
2 tablespoons chili powder
1 teaspoon kosher salt
1 teaspoon freshly ground black pepper
4 cups chicken broth
1 pound smoked turkey sausage, diced
2 14fl oz cans cannellini beans, rinsed
    and drained
1 (4 oz) can chopped mild green chilis
1 cup whipping cream
½ bunch cilantro, chopped
6 oz Monterey Jack cheese, grated
lime wedges

Alternatively, prepare 1½ cup dried cannellini beans (rinsed) in 4 cups water and ¼ teaspoon salt in the electric pressure cooker and cook on high for 25 minutes. Quick release the pressure. Drain and add instead of the canned beans.

1. Press Sauté, adjust it to high heat. Once the pot is hot, heat oil. Add onions and sauté for 3 minutes. Add garlic, cook for another 30 seconds until fragrant.

2. Add ground turkey and cook until brown. Stir in oregano, cumin, cayenne pepper, chili powder, salt and black pepper. Cancel Sauté.

3. Add the following ingredients in order: broth, sausage, beans and green chili. Do not stir.

4. Close and lock the lid, making sure the steam knob is on Sealing/Locked. Pressure cook on high for 10 minutes.

5. Once the pressure cooking is done, quick or natural release the pressure.

6. Press Sauté, adjust it to low heat. Stir in whipping cream and heat through.

7. Serve in individual bowls. Garnish with grated Monterey Jack cheese, chopped cilantro, and lime juice.

Fish Chowder

While travelling in the maritimes and northern Europe, we noticed that everyone has their own version of a fish chowder. I've put the ingredients that I like together in my version I think it's pretty darn good.

Makes 6-8 servings

8 slices thick bacon, ½ inch pieces
2 tablespoons butter
1 onion, chopped
2 carrots, diced
2 pounds small potatoes halved
2 teaspoons dried thyme
2 teaspoons dried parsley
1 bay leaf
1 teaspoons kosher salt
1 teaspoon freshly ground black pepper
4 cups vegetable broth
3 pounds cod, cut into 2 inch pieces
1 cup whipping cream
1 tablespoon fresh Italian parsley, chopped (garnish)

1. Press Sauté, adjust it to high heat. Once the pot is hot, add bacon and render until brown. Remove the bacon and drain on a paper towel.

2. Melt butter, add onion and carrots and sauté for 3 minutes.

3. Add 1 cup vegetable broth to deglaze, scraping up any brown bits from the bottom of the pot. Cancel Sauté.

4. Add potatoes, thyme, parsley, bay leaf, salt and pepper, and remaining vegetable broth.

5. Close and lock the lid, making sure the steam knob is on Sealing/Locked. Pressure cook on high for 5 minutes.

6. Once the pressure cooking is done, quick or natural release the pressure.

7. Press Sauté, adjust it to low heat. Add cod and cook for 3-5 minutes or until cooked through. Add whipping cream and heat through.

8. Serve in individual bowls, garnish with parsley and bacon bits. Enjoy with fresh crusty bread.

Malaysian Seafood Laksa

Makes 4 servings

1 package Teans Gourmet Laksa Paste
6 cups vegetable broth or water
1 can coconut milk
2 stalks lemongrass, bruised
1 package tofu pockets, cut in half
½ pound fish balls
½ pound prawns
½ pound calamari rings
½ pound bean sprouts, blanched
1 cucumber, julienne
4 eggs, medium boiled, cut in half
1 pound thin vermicelli rice noodles, cooked following package instructions

----

1. Press Sauté. In the inner cooking pot, add vegetable broth or water. Heat until simmering, add paste and stir until paste is dissolved completely. Cancel Sauté. Add coconut milk, and lemongrass.

2. Close and lock the lid, making sure the steam knob is on Sealing/Locked. Pressure cook on high for 5 minutes.

3. Once the pressure cooking is done, quick or natural release the pressure.

4. Press Sauté. Add the tofu pockets, fish balls, prawns and calamari and cook through, 2-3 minutes.

5. Assemble each individual bowl with noodles topped with bean sprouts, cucumber, and egg. Distribute the seafood evenly as you pour the soup into the bowls.

Creamy Seafood Chowder

If I see a creamy seafood chowder on the menu, I am likely to order it as it is one of my favourite soups. Since we don't eat out as much these days, I love that I can make this at home and put in whatever seafood I like.

Makes 6-8 servings

1 5 oz can baby clams
8 slices thick bacon, ½ inch pieces
2 tablespoons butter
1 onion, chopped
2 stalks celery, chopped
¼ cup flour
2 pounds small potatoes halved
2 teaspoons dried thyme
2 teaspoons dried parsley
1 bay leaf
1 teaspoon kosher salt
½ teaspoon freshly ground black pepper
4 cups vegetable or fish broth
1 pound cod, cut into 1 inch pieces
1 pound shrimp, shelled and deveined
½ pound scallops
1 cup whipping cream
1 tablespoon fresh Italian parsley,
    chopped (garnish)

Substitute cod with halibut, salmon or other white fish. Shellfish can be substituted with crab, lobster, or mussels. Use what you like!

1. Drain clams, reserve juice and set aside.

2. Press Sauté, adjust it to high heat. Once the pot is hot, add bacon and render until brown. Remove the bacon and drain on a paper towel.

3. Melt butter, add onion and celery and sauté for 3 minutes.

4. Add flour, cook for 1 minute.

5. Add 1 cup vegetable or fish broth to deglaze, scraping up any brown bits from the bottom of the pot. Cancel Sauté.

6. Add potatoes, thyme, parsley, bay leaf, salt and pepper, remaining broth and reserved clam juice.

7. Close and lock the lid, making sure the steam knob is on Sealing/Locked. Pressure cook on high for 5 minutes.

8. Once the pressure cooking is done, quick or natural release the pressure.

9. Press Sauté, adjust it to low heat. Add whipping cream and heat through.

10. Add cod, shrimp, scallops, clams and cook for 2-3 minutes or until cooked through.

11. Serve in individual bowls, garnish with parsley and bacon bits. Enjoy with fresh crusty bread.

Hot and Sour Soup

Hot and sour soup is typically found in northern Chinese restaurants which is a very different style of cooking compared to southern Chinese. The heat from the ginger warms up our insides and I love the balance of savoury, sour and heat. Forget about getting takeout, make it at home!

Makes 6-8 servings

½ oz dried black fungus
1 oz ginger (2 inch knob), sliced
¼ pound cooked ham, ½ inch cubes
6 cups chicken broth
1½ cup savoy cabbage, shredded
1 carrot, julienne
3 green onions, chopped
6-8 fresh Shiitake mushrooms, stems removed, thinly sliced
1 pound medium firm tofu, ½ inch cubes
4 oz bamboo shoots, strips
½ cup rice vinegar
3 tablespoons soy sauce
2 tablespoons cornstarch
2 tablespoons cold water
2 pinches ground white pepper
3 eggs, lightly beaten
1 teaspoon sesame oil

———

1. Rehydrate black fungus by covering with hot water for 30 minutes. Drain and set aside.

2. In the inner cooking pot, add ginger, ham and chicken broth.

3. Close and lock the lid, making sure the steam knob is on Sealing/Locked. Pressure cook on high for 5 minutes.

4. Meanwhile, prepare the rest of the ingredients.

5. Once the pressure cooking is done, quick or natural release the pressure.

6. Remove the slices of ginger.

7. Press Sauté. Add carrots and cabbage and cook for 3 minutes.

8. Add bamboo shoots, green onions, mushrooms, tofu, black fungus, rice vinegar, soy sauce.

9. In a small bowl, dissolve the cornstarch in cold water and stir the slurry into the soup. Simmer until thickened. Add ground white pepper.

10. While gently stirring the soup, slowly drizzle in the eggs to create the egg ribbons. Cancel Sauté.

11. Add sesame oil. Adjust the taste to your liking by adding more vinegar, ground white pepper and/or sesame oil.

Miso Ramen Faster

I tried making authentic miso ramen once and it was so much work, I did not try it again. With this faster version, it is so much simpler but still delicious and much faster to get on the table for dinner.

Makes 4 servings

½ onion, chopped
2 cloves garlic, minced
1 oz ginger (2 inch knob), grated
1 tablespoon vegetable oil
1 pound ground pork
1 tablespoon soy bean paste
¼ cup white miso paste
¼ cup red miso paste
2 tablespoons sugar
2 tablespoons sake
8 cups chicken broth

TO SERVE
1 pound ramen noodles, cooked
¼ cup dried seaweed
½ pound bean sprouts, blanched
1 cup corn, cooked and buttered
4 medium boiled eggs, halved
2 green onions, chopped
roasted sesame seeds

1. Press Sauté. Once the pot is hot, heat oil. Add onion and ginger and sauté for 3 minutes. Add garlic, cook for another 30 seconds until fragrant.

2. Add pork and cook until no longer pink. Cancel Sauté.

3. Stir the three pastes into pork mixture until all the paste is melted. Add sake and chicken broth.

4. Close and lock the lid, making sure the steam knob is on Sealing/Locked. Pressure cook on high for 10 minutes.

5. Meanwhile, prepare the remaining ingredients.

6. Once the pressure cooking is done, quick or natural release the pressure.

7. Assemble each individual bowl with noodles topped with seaweed, bean sprouts, corn, egg, green onion, and sesame seeds. Pour soup over top.

Sausage, Kale and Couscous Soup

Makes 6-8 servings

1 tablespoon olive oil
1 pound ground Italian sausage
1 large onion, chopped
2 carrots, diced
2 stalks celery, chopped
2 cloves garlic, minced
1 teaspoon dried basil
1 bay leaf
2 teaspoons dried parsley
1 teaspoon celery salt
1 teaspoon kosher salt
½ teaspoon freshly ground pepper
Parmesan rind (optional)
6 cups chicken broth
1 cup pearl couscous

1 cup milk
1 cup half and half
1 bunch kale, stems removed and
   chopped
1 teaspoon kosher salt
½ teaspoon freshly ground black pepper
freshly grated Parmesan cheese (optional)

―――――

1. Press Sauté, adjust it to high heat. Once the pot is hot, heat oil. Add sausage and brown until cooked through. Add onion, carrot, celery and sauté for 3 minutes. Add garlic, cook for another 30 seconds until fragrant.

2. Pour in 1 cup broth to deglaze, scraping up any brown bits from the bottom of the pot. Cancel Sauté.

3. Add basil, bay leaf, parsley, celery salt, salt and pepper, Parmesan rind and couscous. Cover with remaining broth.

4. Close and lock the lid, making sure the steam knob is on Sealing/Locked. Pressure cook on high for 10 minutes.

5. Once the pressure cooking is done, quick or natural release the pressure.

6. Press Sauté, adjust it to low heat. Remove bay leaf and Parmesan rind. Add milk and half and half and heat through. Add kale and salt and pepper to taste.

7. Garnish with Parmesan cheese. Serve with fresh crusty bread.

Pork Belly and Sausage Cassoulet

I first tried cassoulet in a French restaurant in Seattle and I was floored by the explosion of flavour in my mouth. Cassoulet originated as peasant food in the southwest region of France, slow-cooked with beans and duck, goose, mutton and/or pork depending on what was available. I decided to try this with pork belly and sausage. So good!

Makes 4-6 servings

4 slices thick bacon, ½ inch pieces
1 pound pork belly, 1½ inch pieces
4 links garlic pork sausage
1 onion, chopped
2 cloves garlic, minced
½ cup dry white wine
1 carrot, 3 inch pieces
2 stalks celery, 3 inch pieces
1 teaspoon kosher salt
½ teaspoon freshly ground black pepper
2 sprigs fresh thyme
4 sprigs fresh Italian parsley
2 bay leaves
¼ cup chicken broth
2 14 fl oz cans cannellini beans, rinsed and drained

———

1. Press Sauté, adjust it to high heat. Once the pot is hot, add bacon and render until brown. Remove the bacon to a large bowl and set aside.

2. Add pork belly and brown on all sides. Remove pork belly and set aside in the large bowl.

3. Add sausage links and brown on all sides. Remove sausage and set aside in the large bowl.

4. Add onions and cook until they start to brown, about 10 minutes. Add garlic, cook for another 30 seconds until fragrant.

5. Add wine to deglaze, scraping up any brown bits from the bottom of the pot. Let cook for 2 minutes. Cancel Sauté.

6. Add meat with their juices, carrot, celery, salt, pepper, thyme, parsley, bay leaves, chicken broth, and beans.

7. Close and lock the lid, making sure the steam knob is on Sealing/Locked. Pressure cook on high for 30 minutes.

8. Once the pressure cooking is done, quick or natural release the pressure.

9. Remove carrot, celery, thyme, parsley and bay leaves. If desired, skim fat and discard.

10. Press Sauté. Cook for another 5-10 minutes until the sauce thickens.

11. Serve with crusty bread to sop up the sauce.

Pork Chile Verde

Mexican food is probably one of my top choices for "if I could only choose one cuisine to live on." This is one of my favourite dishes to make at home because it is full of deep rich flavours that soak into the rice and beans. So delicious!

Makes 6-8 servings

2 poblano peppers
1½ pounds tomatillos, husked and rinsed (approximately 9)
2 onions
4 cloves garlic
½ bunch cilantro, chopped
1 teaspoon chicken bouillon
3 pounds pork shoulder, 1½ inch pieces
1 tablespoon kosher salt, divided
1½ teaspoon freshly ground black pepper, divided
1 cup chicken broth
1 tablespoon oregano
¼ teaspoon cumin

---

1. Preheat broiler. Cut the poblano peppers in half and discard stem and seeds. Remove husks from tomatillos and cut them in half. Cut onions into eighths. Lay the peppers and tomatillos skin side up and scatter onions on the sheet pan. Place the pan under the broiler for 5-7 minutes until sufficiently charred.

2. Place the peppers in a sealed plastic bag and let them steam for 5 minutes. Remove the skin.

3. In a blender, add roasted vegetables, garlic, cilantro, chicken bouillon and purée until smooth.

4. Season pork pieces with 2 teaspoons salt and 1 teaspoon pepper.

5. Press Sauté, adjust it to high heat. Once the pot is hot, heat oil. Add pork and brown for 3 minutes per side. To avoid overcrowding, cook the pork pieces in batches. Remove the pork and set aside. Discard grease.

6. Add chicken broth to deglaze, scraping up any brown bits from the bottom of the pot. Cancel Sauté.

7. Add oregano, cumin, 1 teaspoon salt, ½ teaspoon pepper, and meat. Cover pork with tomatillo mixture. Do not stir.

8. Close and lock the lid, making sure the steam knob is on Sealing/Locked. Pressure cook on high for 35 minutes.

9. Once the pressure cooking is done, quick or natural release the pressure.

10. Serve with rice, beans, salsa, guacamole, and sour cream. You can also use the chile to make burritos or tacos.

French Onion Soup

When I was pregnant with my second, I was craving French onion soup. I found a French bistro in town that had great reviews of their onion soup. When I arrived with my then one-year old, I caught the look of horror on the restaurant owner's face. It turned out she was afraid my baby would be the messy, screaming kind disrupting her customers in business suits. Good thing my daughter is super chill and well behaved in restaurants. To this day, she enjoys good food as much as anyone. We were asked to come back anytime.

Makes 4-6 servings

¼ cup unsalted butter
2 tablespoons olive oil
4 large sweet onions, sliced
pinch baking soda
½ cup sherry or dry red wine
6 cups beef broth
2 sprigs fresh thyme
1½ teaspoon kosher salt
½ teaspoon freshly ground black pepper
4-6 thick slices rustic country bread, toasted
1 cup grated Gruyère cheese
1 cup grated mozzarella cheese
1 tablespoon Italian parsley, chopped

———————

1. Press Sauté. Once the pot is hot, heat oil and melt butter. Add onions and a good pinch of baking soda. Cook for 5 minutes. Press Cancel.

2. Close and lock the lid, making sure the steam knob is on Sealing/Locked. Pressure cook on high for 15 minutes.

3. Once the pressure cooking is done, quick release the pressure.

4. Drain onions, reserving the liquid. Return onions to the pot.

5. Press Sauté, adjust it to low heat. Cook until moisture has completely evaporated and onions caramelize, stirring frequently, about 10 minutes.

6. Once onion is golden brown and significantly reduced, add the sherry or wine to deglaze, scraping up any brown bits from the bottom of the pot. Add broth, reserved liquid from onions, thyme, salt and pepper. Press Cancel.

7. Close and lock the lid, making sure the steam knob is on Sealing/Locked. Pressure cook on high for 5 minutes.

8. Meanwhile, preheat broiler. Top each slice of toasted bread with an even amount of gruyère and mozzarella. Place under broiler for 3-5 minutes until cheese is melted and slightly browned.

9. Once the pressure cooking is done, quick release the pressure.

10. Ladle soup into individual bowls and top with cheese bread. Garnish with parsley.

Leek and Potato Soup

Every now and then I love me some smooth creamy soup. Usually I prefer rustic and chunky but not for leek and potato. It has to be blended until super smooth and creamy where all the flavours just come together and burst with every spoonful.

Makes 6-8 servings

¾ pound bacon, cut into small pieces
2 pounds leeks (white and light green parts only), chopped
3 cloves garlic, minced
3 large russet potatoes, 1 inch cubes
3-4 sprigs fresh thyme or 1 teaspoon dried thyme
1 bay leaf
2 teaspoons kosher salt
1 teaspoon freshly ground pepper
6 cups chicken broth
1 cup whipping cream
1 tablespoon Italian parsley, chopped (garnish)

———

1. Press Sauté, adjust it to high heat. Once the pot is hot, add bacon and render until brown. Remove the bacon and drain on a paper towel. Discard most of the bacon fat, leaving approximately 3 tablespoons.

2. Press Cancel and then press Sauté again. Add chopped leeks to the pot and cook them for 5-7 minutes, stirring occasionally. Add garlic, cook for another 30 seconds until fragrant. Add 1 cup of broth to deglaze, scraping up any brown bits from the bottom of the pot. Cancel Sauté.

3. Add potatoes, thyme, bay leaf, salt and pepper. Cover with chicken broth.

4. Close and lock the lid, making sure the steam knob is on Sealing/Locked. Pressure cook on high for 10 minutes.

5. Once the pressure cooking is done, quick or natural release the pressure.

6. Remove the thyme sprigs and bay leaf. Using an immersion blender, blend until smooth.

7. Press Sauté, adjust it to low heat. Add the whipping cream and heat through.

8. Serve in individual bowls, garnish with parsley and bacon bits. Enjoy with fresh crusty bread.

Roasted Tomato Soup

Roasting the tomatoes adds an elevated flavour profile that you are sure to enjoy. This soup goes perfect with grilled cheese sandwiches.

Makes 4 servings

2 pounds tomatoes
1 tablespoon olive oil
1 teaspoon kosher salt
¼ teaspoon freshly ground black pepper
1 tablespoon butter
1 tablespoon olive oil
1 onion, sliced
3 cloves garlic, minced
¼ cup fresh basil, chopped

pinch dried thyme
pinch dried oregano
1 teaspoon balsamic crema or
    1 tablespoon balsamic vinegar
2 cups chicken broth
1 teaspoon kosher salt
½ teaspoon freshly ground black pepper
croutons (garnish)
extra-virgin olive oil (garnish)

1. Cut tomatoes in half and remove the stem. Place in a single layer of an air fryer basket, season with ½ teaspoon salt and ⅛ teaspoon pepper and drizzle lightly with olive oil. Add a second layer and repeat.

2. Set the temperature at 350°F on the air fryer for 20 minutes. Alternatively, roast tomatoes in a single layer on a sheet pan in the oven, preheated to 425°F, for 35 minutes.

3. Press Sauté, adjust it to high heat. Once the pot is hot, heat oil and melt butter. Add onion and sauté for about 10 minute until onion starts to brown. Add garlic, cook for another 30 seconds until fragrant. Cancel Sauté.

4. Once roasted tomatoes are done, add them to the pressure cooker including the juices at the bottom of the air fryer. Add the basil, thyme, oregano, balsamic crema or vinegar and chicken broth. Season with salt and pepper.

5. Close and lock the lid, making sure the steam knob is on Sealing/Locked. Pressure cook on high for 5 minutes.

6. Once the pressure cooking is done, quick or natural release the pressure.

7. Using an immersion blender, blend until smooth.

8. Serve in individual bowls, garnish with croutons and a drizzle of extra virgin olive oil.

Cheesy Broccoli Soup

This broccoli and cheese soup is a great way to get in all your veggies in a bowl full of yummy goodness. Even the kids will gobble it up! Actually, my kids will gobble anything up if you put cheese on it.

Makes 4-6 servings

¼ cup butter
2 medium onion, diced
2 cloves garlic, minced
¼ cup flour
2 carrots, shredded
4 cups broccoli florets, chopped
4 cups chicken broth
¼ cup freshly grated Parmesan
1 teaspoon kosher salt
½ teaspoon freshly ground black pepper
1 cup whipping cream
8 oz mild cheddar cheese, shredded

Substitute chicken broth with vegetable broth for a vegetarian version.

1. Press Sauté. Once the pot is hot, melt butter. Add onion and sauté for 3 minutes. Add garlic, cook for another 30 seconds until fragrant. Add flour, cook for another minute.

2. Add 1 cup broth to deglaze, scraping up any brown bits from the bottom of the pot. Cancel Sauté.

3. Add carrot, broccoli and remaining chicken broth. Season with salt and pepper.

4. Close and lock the lid, making sure the steam knob is on Sealing/Locked. Pressure cook on high for 2 minutes.

5. Once the pressure cooking is done, quick release the pressure.

6. Press Sauté, adjust it to low heat. When the soup begins to simmer, add cream until heated through. Stir in cheeses until melted.

7. Serve in individual bowls with crusty bread.

Corn and Potato Chowder

In the summer, I like to use fresh corn and warba potatoes but who really wants soup in the heat of summer? Still quite tasty when using frozen corn and white or red potatoes.

Makes 4-6 servings

8 slices thick bacon, ½ inch pieces
2 tablespoons butter
1 onion, chopped
2 carrots, diced
2 pounds small potatoes halved
2 cups corn, fresh or frozen
4 cups chicken broth
2 teaspoons dried thyme
1 bay leaf
1 cup whipping cream
2 teaspoons kosher salt
1 teaspoon freshly ground black pepper
1 tablespoon fresh Italian parsley, chopped (garnish)

———

1. Press Sauté, adjust it to high heat. Once the pot is hot, add bacon and render until brown. Remove the bacon and drain on a paper towel.

2. Melt butter, add onion and carrots and sauté for 3 minutes.

3. Add 1 cup chicken broth to deglaze, scraping up any brown bits from the bottom of the pot. Cancel Sauté.

4. Add potatoes, corn, thyme, bay leaf and remaining chicken broth.

5. Close and lock the lid, making sure the steam knob is on Sealing/Locked. Pressure cook on high for 5 minutes.

6. Once the pressure cooking is done, quick or natural release the pressure.

7. Press Sauté, adjust it to low heat. Add whipping cream and heat through.

8. Serve in individual bowls, garnish with parsley and bacon bits. Enjoy with fresh crusty bread.

Cream of Mushroom

When I think of cream of mushroom, I think Campbell's. I was a pro at making it out of a can as a young child. But now that I'm all grown up and have found that I don't have to eat it out of a can, well… this is what I came up with for a delicious bowl of cream of mushroom.

Makes 4-6 servings

1-2 tablespoons olive oil
1 pound cremini mushrooms, quartered
1 pound white mushrooms, quartered
½ teaspoon kosher salt
¼ teaspoon freshly ground black pepper
1 onion, diced
3 stalks celery, diced
1 leek, white part only, sliced
3 cloves garlic, minced
½ cup dry white wine
2 sprigs fresh thyme
2 bay leaves
4 cups chicken broth
1 teaspoon kosher salt
½ teaspoon freshly ground black pepper
½ pound wild mushrooms, sliced
1 tablespoon olive oil
pinch kosher salt
pinch dried thyme
⅛ teaspoon freshly ground black pepper
1 cup whipping cream
¼ cup Italian parsley, chopped

1. Press Sauté, adjust it to high heat. Once the pot is hot, heat olive oil. In small batches, brown mushrooms on one side without stirring for 2 minutes or until golden brown. Season with salt and pepper. Remove into a bowl and repeat with remaining mushrooms. Adding more olive oil as necessary. Set mushrooms aside.

2. Add more olive oil to the pot, if needed. Add onions, celery, and leek. Sauté for 5-7 minutes until browned. Add garlic, cook for another 30 seconds until fragrant.

3. Pour in the wine to deglaze, scraping up any brown bits from the bottom of the pot. Cook for 2 minutes. Cancel Sauté.

4. Add thyme, bay leaves, chicken broth, salt and pepper and mushrooms.

5. Close and lock the lid, making sure the steam knob is on Sealing/Locked. Pressure cook on high for 10 minutes.

6. Meanwhile, preheat oven to 400°F.

7. In a medium bowl, toss wild mushrooms with olive oil, pinch of salt, pinch of dried thyme and ⅛ teaspoon freshly ground black pepper. Spread mushrooms evenly on a sheet pan and roast for 10-12 minutes, until mushrooms are golden brown. Remove from oven and set aside.

8. Once the pressure cooking is done, quick or natural release the pressure.

9. Remove the thyme sprigs and bay leaves.

10. Using an immersion blender, blend until smooth.

11. Press Sauté, adjust it to low heat. Add the whipping cream, roasted wild mushrooms and parsley and heat through.

12. Serve in individual bowls.

Mains

BBQ Beef Ribs

Beef Rendang

Korean Galbi Saucy Beef Short Ribs

Tomato Sausage Pasta

Teriyaki Beef and Tofu

Basic Asian Chicken

Hainanese Chicken Legs and Rice

Hawaiian Style Ribs

Black Bean Spare Ribs

Mom's Chinese Ribs

Pulled Pork

Tawainese Braised Pork Belly

Steamed Pork Patty

Country Shrimp Boil

BBQ Beef Ribs

While BBQ pork ribs have been a standard item in our family menu, I have never tried making BBQ beef ribs. I made the ribs two ways, half with BBQ sauce, the other half with just the rub. They were both delicious, with Dude preferring the dry rub version.

Makes 3 servings

6 large beef ribs

DRY RUB
4 tablespoons brown sugar
1 tablespoon kosher salt
1½ teaspoon paprika
½ teaspoon freshly ground black pepper
¼ teaspoon thyme
¼ teaspoon onion powder
¼ teaspoon garlic powder

If you prefer barbecue sauce, before placing ribs under the broiler, brush ribs with your favourite barbecue sauce.

---

1. In a small bowl, combine all the dry rub ingredients and mix well. Place ribs and dry rub in a large resealable bag and shake. Massage the rub into the ribs and refrigerate for at least 30 minutes.

2. Place a trivet in the inner cooking pot and add 1 cup water. Place ribs on top of the trivet.

3. Close and lock the lid, making sure the steam knob is on Sealing/Locked. Pressure cook on high for 30 minutes.

4. Once the pressure cooking is done, quick release the pressure.

5. Preheat broiler. Line a sheet pan with parchment paper or aluminum foil and place the ribs in a single layer, meat side up.

6. Place the ribs under the broiler for 3-5 minutes until caramelized.

Beef Rendang

When we crave Malaysian flavours, we take short cuts all the time by using a packaged paste. Malaysian cooking can be very time consuming and complicated, especially when a lot of the ingredients are not always readily available. I'm thankful that my mother-in-law found some really good pastes. If they're good enough for her (she used to make all her pastes from scratch), then they're definitely good enough for me!

Makes 6-8 servings

1 tablespoon vegetable oil
2 shallots chopped
3 cloves garlic, minced
1 package Tean's Gourmet Rendang Paste
½ cup water
3 pounds boneless beef short-ribs, cut into 2 inch pieces
1 14 fl oz can coconut milk
1 tablespoon cilantro, chopped (garnish)

---

1. Press Sauté. Once the pot is hot, heat oil. Add shallots and sauté for about 3 minutes. Add garlic, cook for another 30 seconds until fragrant.

2. Add paste and cook for about 3-4 minutes.

3. Add water to deglaze, scraping up any brown bits from the bottom of the pot. Cancel Sauté.

4. Stir in beef, making sure the pieces are covered in the paste.

5. Add coconut milk and do NOT stir.

6. Close and lock the lid, making sure the steam knob is on Sealing/Locked. Pressure cook on high for 30 minutes.

7. Once the pressure cooking is done, quick release the pressure.

8. Press Sauté, adjust it to high heat. Cook until the curry browns and liquid is reduced, approximately 30 minutes.

9. Serve with rice.

Korean Galbi Saucy Beef Short Ribs

One of my favourite meals and it's so easy to make. Sometimes I cheat and just use a bottled sauce but making your own sauces at home ensures you know exactly what is going into your meal. This sauce uses the basic Asian sauces you may already have in your pantry. Hope you'll give it a try and see how easy it is to make.

Makes 4-6 servings

½ onion
6 cloves garlic
½ oz ginger (1 inch knob), peeled
½ Asian pear, peeled and cored
¼ cup water
½ cup brown sugar
½ cup soy sauce
2 tablespoons Mirin
2 tablespoons sesame oil
¼ teaspoon black pepper
3 pounds beef short-ribs, flanken or Korean LA cut
1 tablespoon cornstarch
1 tablespoon cold water
1 tablespoon roasted sesame,
1 green onion, chopped

———

1. In a blender, add onion, garlic, ginger, Asian pear, and water and puree until smooth.

2. Add brown sugar, soy sauce, mirin, sesame oil and black pepper and blend on a lower setting until well combined.

3. In the inner cooking pot, place half the ribs and pour half the sauce over ribs. Repeat with remaining ribs and sauce.

4. Close and lock the lid, making sure the steam knob is on Sealing/Locked. Pressure cook on high for 5 minutes.

5. Once the pressure cooking is done, quick release the pressure.

6. Preheat the broiler. Line a sheet pan with foil or parchment paper and place the ribs in a single layer.

7. Place the ribs under the broiler for 3-5 minutes. Turn them over and broil for another 3-5 minutes.

8. Press Sauté, adjust it to low heat. In a small bowl, dissolve the cornstarch in cold water and stir the slurry into the sauce. Simmer until thickened.

9. Cut the ribs up into smaller segments and put them back in the sauce and stir to cover.

10. Garnish with roasted sesame and chopped green onion.

11. Serve with Japanese rice and kimchi and/or other Korean sides.

Tomato Sausage Pasta

I rarely cook the same dish more than once a month but this one makes it into the menu rotation about once a week. It's fast, easy and we all love it.

Makes 4-6 servings

1 tablespoon olive oil
1 medium onion, chopped
3 cloves garlic, minced
1 pound ground sweet Italian sausage
3 cups beef broth or water
1 pound pasta
24 fl oz jar favourite tomato pasta sauce
¼ cup fresh basil, chiffonade
¼ cup grated Parmesan cheese
freshly ground black pepper

———

1. Press Sauté. Once the pot is hot, heat olive oil. Add onion and sauté for 3 minutes. Add garlic, cook for another 30 seconds until fragrant. Add sausage and cook until browned.

2. Pour in 1 cup beef broth to deglaze, scraping up any brown bits from the bottom of the pot. Cancel Sauté.

3. Add the pasta. Pour remaining beef broth over the pasta. If you are using spaghetti, try to fan out the noodles so that it looks like pick-up sticks to minimize the clumping of the pasta.

4. Evenly cover the pasta with the pasta sauce. Do not stir.

5. Close and lock the lid, making sure the steam knob is on Sealing/Locked. Pressure cook on high for half the amount of cook time stated on the package of pasta. (i.e. if the packages says to cook for 8-9 minutes, set the pressure cooker for 4 minutes.)

6. Once the pressure cooking is done, quick release the pressure. The pasta will look soupy. Give the pasta a good stir and the pasta will absorb the rest of the liquid.

7. Serve on individual plates. Garnish with basil, Parmesan and black pepper. Enjoy immediately.

Teriyaki Beef and Tofu

Before I started eating sushi, this is what I would order at a Japanese restaurant, along with a Coke. I'm not sure why, it was just what I liked. When I eat out at Japanese restaurants nowadays, it's all about the sushi but I will make this at home and no, I no longer need to enjoy it with a Coke.

Makes 4-6 servings

1 pound flank steak, thinly sliced
1 tablespoon cornstarch
1 tablespoon canola oil
1 clove garlic, minced
1 teaspoon ginger, grated
¼ cup soy sauce
2 tablespoons Mirin
2 teaspoons rice vinegar
1 tablespoon brown sugar
½ teaspoon sesame oil
1 pound medium firm tofu, cut into 1 inch cubes
1 tablespoon cornstarch
1 tablespoon water

———————

1. In a medium bowl, mix the steak with cornstarch.

2. Press Sauté, adjust it to high heat. Once the pot is hot, heat oil. Add beef and stir fry until mostly cooked through.

3. Cancel Sauté. Add ginger, garlic, soy sauce, Mirin, rice vinegar, brown sugar and sesame oil and stir. Gently place the tofu cubes on top.

4. Close and lock the lid, making sure the steam knob is on Sealing/Locked. Pressure cook on high for 5 minutes.

5. Once the pressure cooking is done, quick release the pressure.

6. Press Sauté, adjust it to low heat. In a small bowl, dissolve the cornstarch in cold water and stir the slurry into the sauce. Simmer until thickened.

7. Serve with Jasmine rice.

Basic Asian Chicken

This basic Asian chicken is so simple and versatile. It's great for Asian style salads and sandwiches when a barbecue rotisserie chicken just won't do.

Makes 8 cups

8 whole chicken legs
2 teaspoon kosher salt
6-8 green onions
3 oz ginger (4 inch knob), peeled
   and sliced
5 cloves garlic, bruised
kosher salt

This recipe is used in the Malaysian Chicken Laksa on page 34 and Hainanese Chicken and Rice on page 88.

---

1. Season chicken with kosher salt.

2. Place a trivet in the inner cooking pot and add 1 cup water. Loosely layer chicken, green onion, ginger and garlic on top of the trivet.

3. Close and lock the lid, making sure the steam knob is on Sealing/Locked. Pressure cook on high for 15 minutes.

4. Once the pressure cooking is done, quick release the pressure.

5. Remove the chicken and place in a large bowl of ice water for about 10 minutes. This will stop the cooking.

6. Shred the chicken to use in salads, sandwiches and wraps.

7. Remove the trivet and discard the remaining ingredients. Pour the broth into a bowl and skim off the fat. Save the broth to use in other meals by refrigerating or freezing in an airtight container.

Hainanese Chicken Legs and Rice

If you ask my kids what kind of chicken they want for dinner, this will always be their first choice but they call it white skin chicken. This is perfect hot weather food because the chicken is served at room temperature. This is one of our favourite dishes and so simple to make. Hope you will enjoy it too!

Makes 4-6 servings

1 Basic Asian Chicken recipe (page 87)
3 rice cups Jasmine rice
3 cloves garlic, minced
3 rice cups reserved chicken broth
3 green onions, chopped
2 oz ginger (2 inch knob), grated
¼ teaspoon kosher salt

2 tablespoons vegetable oil
1 English cucumber, sliced
2-3 pinches ground white pepper
2 tablespoons soy sauce
2 tablespoons sesame oil
8 sprigs cilantro

1. Make Basic Asian Chicken recipe.

2. Rinse the rice until the water runs clear and place in the same inner cooking pot after making the chicken. Add garlic and reserved chicken broth. If there is not enough chicken broth, add more water.

3. Close and lock the lid, making sure the steam knob is on Sealing/Locked. Pressure cook on high for 4 minutes.

4. Once the pressure cooking is done, natural pressure release for 10 minutes and then quick release the remaining pressure.

5. Meanwhile, place the green onion, ginger and salt into a small bowl. In a frying pan, heat up the oil until you see a whisp of white smoke. Pour it over the green onion and ginger mixture and mix well.

6. Lay the cucumber slices down on a serving plate. Once the chicken is cool enough to handle, separate the meat from the bones, slice or shred the chicken and place on top of the cucumber. Sprinkle with 2-3 pinches of ground white pepper.

7. In a small bowl, stir the soy sauce and sesame oil until well mixed. Drizzle the mixture evenly over the chicken. Garnish with cilantro leaves.

8. Serve with rice and green onion mixture on the side.

Hawaiian Style Ribs

I wanted something different from our usual barbecue sauced pork ribs and came up with this pineapple version. There's just something about sweetness with pork that goes so well together. This is now one of the kids' favourite meals.

Makes 4-6 servings

2 racks pork back ribs
3 oz ginger (4 inch knob), 1 tablespoon grated; remaining sliced
1 onion, cut into eighths
2 teaspoons kosher salt
1 19 fl oz can crushed pineapple
1 cup chicken broth

½ cup brown sugar
1 tablespoon dark soy sauce
3 tablespoons soy sauce
2 tablespoons oyster sauce
1 tablespoon cornstarch
1 tablespoon cold water

1. Remove the silver skin from the back of two racks of pork back ribs and cut the ribs into 3-4 rib sections. Season the ribs front and back with 2 teaspoons salt.

2. In the inner cooking pot, add 1 cup water and layer ribs, ginger and onion.

3. Close and lock the lid, making sure the steam knob is on Sealing/Locked. Pressure cook on high for 18 minutes. If you like the ribs less fall-off-the-bone, with a little tug on then, cook them for only 15 minutes. If you want them to completely fall off the bone, cook 20 minutes.

4. Meanwhile, in a medium saucepan, add pineapple, broth, sugar, dark soy sauce, soy sauce, oyster sauce and ginger. Bring to a simmer on medium heat and let it simmer for 30 minutes.

5. In a small bowl, dissolve the cornstarch in cold water and stir the slurry into the sauce. Simmer until thickened. Remove from heat and set aside.

6. Once the pressure cooking is done, quick release the pressure.

7. Preheat the broiler. Line a sheet pan with parchment paper or aluminum foil. Lay the ribs, bone side up and cover with half the sauce. Place under the broiler for 3-5 minutes until the sauce is caramelized. Repeat on the other side but broil them for 7-9 minutes.

8. Serve with the caramelized sauce from the pan.

Black Bean Spare Ribs

Another childhood favourite that we enjoyed as kids for dinner but Dude's family only ordered this at dim sum. I find it fascinating that every family has different memories of the same dish. I remember how my mom used to grind the black beans and garlic in a bowl with the handle of her cleaver. I don't do that since I just mince the black beans and garlic.

Makes 2-3 servings

1 tablespoon vegetable oil
1 tablespoon ShaoHsing wine
1 tablespoon soy sauce
2 teaspoons sugar
1 teaspoon sesame oil
¼ teaspoon salt
1 tablespoon cornstarch
1 pound pork spare ribs or side ribs, cut crosswise into 1-1½ inch pieces
½ oz ginger (1 inch knob), grated
3 cloves garlic, minced
1 tablespoon fermented black beans, minced
1 green onion, chopped (garnish)

———————

1. In a medium mixing bowl, add the oil, wine, soy sauce, sugar, sesame oil, salt and cornstarch and mix well. Add the spare ribs and mix well, making sure all the pieces are coated. Add ginger, garlic and black beans and stir well. Let marinate for at least 30 minutes or up to overnight.

2. Put the spare ribs into a shallow oven safe dish with a 1-2 inch lip because the ribs will produce a lot of sauce.

3. Place a trivet in the inner cooking pot and add 1 cup water. Place the plate of spare ribs on the trivet.

4. Close and lock the lid, making sure the steam knob is on Sealing/Locked. Pressure cook on high for 15 minutes.

5. Once the pressure cooking is done, quick release the pressure.

6. Carefully remove the dish from the pot. Garnish with green onion.

7. Serve with Jasmine rice.

Mom's Chinese Ribs

When I first moved away from home, I remember calling my mom for this recipe. I still have the scrap piece of paper I jotted it down on. Making it in the electric pressure cooker makes this a cinch to cook.

Makes 3-4 servings

1 rack pork side ribs
¼ cup dark soy sauce
¼ cup vinegar
1½ tablespoon rice wine
¼ cup sugar
1½ teaspoon kosher salt
4 cloves garlic, minced
¼ cup water
1 tablespoon cilantro, chopped

———

1. Remove the silver skin from the back ribs and cut into individual bone segments. Place them in the inner cooking pot.

2. In a small bowl, combine dark soy sauce, vinegar, rice wine, sugar, salt, and garlic. Pour evenly over the ribs. Add water.

3. Close and lock the lid, making sure the steam knob is on Sealing/Locked. Pressure cook on high for 15 minutes.

4. Once the pressure cooking is done, quick release the pressure.

5. Press Sauté. Simmer for 2 minutes until ribs are evenly brown.

6. Garnish with chopped cilantro. Serve with rice.

Pulled Pork

The last few times I have ordered sandwiches in a restaurant, I have been quite impressed by the balance of flavours: sweet, sour, spicy and savory; as well as the mouthfeel of textures that made each sandwich incredibly delectable. This is what I am aiming for here with this pulled pork recipe. I hope you will find it as enjoyable as we did.

Makes 6-8 servings

2 pounds pork shoulder, 2 inch pieces
1 tablespoon kosher salt
1 teaspoon freshly ground black pepper
2 tablespoons olive oil
3 cloves garlic
2 tablespoons bourbon
½ cup chicken broth
1½ cup favourite barbecue sauce

COLESLAW
½ head cabbage, core removed and shredded
¼ cup mayonnaise
¼ cup sour cream
1 green onion, chopped
2 tablespoons cilantro, chopped
½ jalapeno pepper, core removed and seeded
1 clove garlic, bruised
1 lime, juiced
¼ teaspoon kosher salt
¼ teaspoon freshly ground pepper
6 brioche or soft hamburger buns
sweet pickles

———

1. Season pork pieces with salt and pepper.

2. Press Sauté, adjust it to high heat. Once the pot is hot, heat oil. In small batches, brown the pork on each side without overcrowding. Remove the pork and place in a bowl.

3. Add 3 cloves garlic, cook for another 30 seconds until fragrant. Add bourbon and ¼ cup chicken broth to deglaze, scraping up any brown bits from the bottom of the pot. Cancel Sauté.

4. Add remaining ¼ cup chicken broth, pork and any remaining jus.

5. Cover the pork with your favourite barbecue sauce. Do not stir.

6. Close and lock the lid, making sure the steam knob is on Sealing/Locked. Pressure cook on high for 45 minutes.

7. Meanwhile, make the coleslaw. Put the shredded cabbage into a large mixing bowl.

8. In a blender, add mayonnaise, sour cream, green onion, cilantro, jalapeno pepper (include seeds if you want it spicier), garlic, lime juice, salt and pepper and blend until smooth. Pour dressing over cabbage and mix well. Refrigerate until ready to use.

9. Once the pressure cooking is done, quick or natural release the pressure.

10. Remove the pork pieces into a large bowl. Discard the garlic, if desired.

11. Press Sauté, adjust it to high heat and reduce the sauce by half until thickened, approximately 10 minutes.

12. Using two forks, shred the pork. Stir in enough sauce until meat is nicely covered but not drowning in sauce.

13. Serve pulled pork on brioche buns or soft hamburger buns, topped with coleslaw and sweet pickles.

Tawainese Braised Pork Belly

This is one of my favourite dishes to make with pork belly. When done right, the pork belly just melts in your mouth. I think cooked lettuce is the best vegetable to go with this as it soaks up the sauce.

Makes 4-6 servings

2 tablespoons vegetable oil
1 small onion, chopped
2 pounds skin-on pork belly cut into ½ inch slices
3 cloves garlic, chopped
¼ cup ShaoHsing wine
1 tablespoon soy sauce
1 tablespoon dark soy sauce
2 tablespoon oyster sauce
1 stick cinnamon
1 bay leaf
2 tablespoons rock sugar
2 star anise
1 oz ginger (2 inch knob), sliced
¼ cup water
2 teaspoons salt
1 tablespoon vegetable oil
1 head green leaf lettuce
1 tablespoon cilantro, chopped (garnish)

---

1. Press Sauté, adjust it to high heat. Once the pot is hot, heat oil. Add onions and sauté for 10 minutes until browned.

2. Add the pork belly and cook for about 10 minutes until browned. Stir in garlic. Cancel Sauté.

3. Add Shao Hsing wine, soy sauce, dark soy sauce, oyster sauce, cinnamon stick, bay leaf, rock sugar, star anise, ginger and water.

4. Close and lock the lid, making sure the steam knob is on Sealing/Locked. Pressure cook on high for 30 minutes.

5. Meanwhile, boil water in a medium pot. Add salt and a tablespoon vegetable oil to the water, then blanch lettuce for 1 minute. Drain and set aside.

6. Once the pressure cooking is done, quick or natural release the pressure.

7. Skim the fat and discard.

8. Press Sauté. Cook for another 5 minutes until the sauce thickens and the pork is evenly brown in colour. Remove the star anise, bay leaf and cinnamon stick.

9. Evenly spread lettuce out on a serving platter. Spoon the pork belly with the sauce over top the lettuce. Garnish with cilantro.

10. Serve with Jasmine rice.

Steamed Pork Patty

This is one of my childhood favourites that my siblings and I would fight over who got to "lick" the plate. Once the meat was all gone, there was always a bit of sauce left and we would call dibs on the plate to have one last scoop of rice to soak it all up.

Makes 4 servings

1 pound lean ground pork
1 tablespoon soy sauce
1 teaspoon kosher salt
1 teaspoon ShaoHsing wine
1 tablespoon sugar
⅛ teaspoon ground white pepper
½ teaspoon sesame oil
1 tablespoon cornstarch

1. In a medium bowl, add pork, soy sauce, salt, Shao Hsing wine, sugar, white pepper and sesame oil. Stir in one direction until the texture is sticky and comes together.

2. Add cornstarch and stir until the corn starch is absorbed into the meat mixture.

3. Divide mixture in half. Gently press one half into a ¾ inch thick patty in a shallow dish with a 1-2 inch lip that is oven safe because the patty will produce a lot of sauce. Repeat with the other half.

4. Place a trivet in the inner cooking pot and add 1 cup of water. Stack the dishes, if you are able, otherwise cook separately.

5. Close and lock the lid, making sure the steam knob is on Sealing/Locked. Pressure cook on high for 15 minutes.

6. Once the pressure cooking is done, quick release the pressure.

7. Carefully remove the dish from the pot.

8. Serve with Jasmine rice.

Country Shrimp Boil

This is such a fun and easy meal to have at home. You can also use Old Bay seasoning to make this even easier but I make my own "Old Bay" seasoning mix and it's still ready in no time. My kids love to dip anything into seasoning, so this is a big hit with them!

Makes 4 servings

SEASONING
1 tablespoon celery salt
2 teaspoons thyme
2 teaspoons smoked paprika
1 teaspoon ground Black Pepper
1 teaspoon ground mustard
⅛ teaspoon allspice
¼ teaspoon crushed red chili flakes
1 pinch ground cinnamon
1 pinch ground nutmeg
1 pinch ground ginger
1 pinch ground cardamom

SHRIMP BOIL
1 bay leaf
½ onion, sliced
½ cup water
1½ pound nugget potatoes, quartered
3 ears corn, cut in thirds
2 tablespoons seasoning mix
1 teaspoon kosher salt
1 pound smoked pork sausage, 1½ inch pieces
½ lemon
1 pound large shrimp, deveined and peeled
¼ teaspoon kosher salt

GARLIC BUTTER
¼ cup salted butter, melted
1-2 cloves garlic, minced

1. In a small bowl, stir all the seasoning ingredients together until well mixed.

2. In a large mixing bowl, add potatoes, corn and toss with 2 tablespoons seasoning and salt.

3. In the inner cooking pot, add water, onion and bay leaf. Place a trivet on top and pour in potatoes and corn. Add sausage and squeeze lemon over top and toss the rind in as well.

4. Close and lock the lid, making sure the steam knob is on Sealing/Locked. Pressure cook on high for 5 minutes.

5. Meanwhile, make the garlic butter. In a small pot on medium heat, melt butter. Add garlic, cook for another 30 seconds until fragrant. Remove from heat and set aside.

6. In the same large mixing bowl, add shrimp and toss with 1 teaspoon seasoning and ¼ teaspoon salt. Set aside.

7. Once the pressure cooking is done, quick release the pressure.

8. Add shrimp and put the lid back on for 1-2 minutes or until shrimp is just cooked through from the residual heat.

9. Drain the contents. Pour mixture onto a sheet pan. Remove bay leaf and lemon rind. Season with remaining seasoning.

10. Serve with garlic butter for dipping and lemon wedges.

Desserts

Caramel Apple Cheesecake
Matcha Cheesecake with Shortbread Crust
Croissant Bread Pudding
Lemon Curd

Caramel Apple Cheesecake

Two of my favourite desserts in one: Apple Crumble and Cheesecake. What's not to love?

Makes 6 servings

OAT CRUMBLE CRUST
¾ cup flour
¾ cup oats
½ cup brown sugar
½ cup melted butter

CHEESECAKE FILLING
8 oz cream cheese, room temperature
½ cup sugar
1 cup sour cream, room temperature
1 egg, room temperature
zest of 1 lemon
2 tablespoons lemon juice
1 teaspoon vanilla extract

CARAMEL SAUCE AND APPLE TOPPING
½ cup sugar
2 tablespoons water
⅓ cup whipping cream
2 tablespoons butter, small pieces
1 tablespoon butter
2 Granny Smith apples, skin and core removed, thinly sliced
¼ lemon, juiced
¼ cup brown sugar

1. Preheat oven to 350°F. Line the bottom of a 7 x 3 inch springform pan with parchment paper.

2. In a medium bowl, combine flour, oats, brown sugar. Add butter and mix until crumbly.

3. Press crumb mixture firmly into the bottom of the pan and slightly up the sides. Bake in preheated oven for 12-15 minutes until golden brown.

4. Let the crust cool for at least 5 minutes before adding cheesecake filling.

5. With an electric mixer on medium, beat cream cheese until smooth. With the mixer on, add sugar in a steady stream.

6. For the next few steps, only mix for 3o seconds and make sure to scrape down the side after the addition of each ingredient.

    •   Add ½ cup sour cream, mix for 3o seconds and scrape the sides of the bowl down. Repeat with remaining sour cream.
    •   Add egg.
    •   Add lemon zest and vanilla.

7. Pour the batter into the cooled crust. Tap pan on work surface to remove any air bubbles. Cover tightly with foil or with a silicone lid.

8. Place a trivet in the inner cooking pot and add 1 cup of water. Place the covered cheesecake on top of the trivet.

9. Close and lock the lid, making sure the steam knob is on Sealing/Locked. Pressure cook on high for 35 minutes.

10. Once the pressure cooking is done, natural pressure release for 10 minutes and then quick release the remaining pressure.

11. The cheesecake should be mostly set, with only the center slightly jiggly.

12. Remove the pan and let it cool for an hour and refrigerate overnight or for at least 4 hours.

13. In a small pot on medium heat, add sugar and water. Cook until the sugar is completely dissolved. Once it starts to boil, increase the heat to medium/high and let it boil until the liquid becomes dark amber in colour. This will take about 4-8 minutes. Whisk in whipping cream. Remove from heat. Drop in pieces of butter, one at a time until melted, into the caramel while whisking constantly. Pour caramel into a bowl. It will thicken as it cools.

14. In a frying pan over medium heat, melt butter. Sauté apples for 5 minutes or until desired texture. Squeeze lemon juice over the apples and add brown sugar. Cook until sugar is dissolved. Remove from pan and let it cool down to room temperature.

15. Assemble the cheesecake. Run a knife along the edge of the cheesecake and transfer it onto a serving plate. Top with caramel sauce and apple slices.

Matcha Cheesecake with Shortbread Crust

I made this recipe when I was looking for an Asian inspired cheesecake. Matcha works really well here, especially with the shortbread crust.

Makes 6 servings

SHORTBREAD CRUST
½ cup butter, room temperature
¼ cup sugar
1 cup flour

CHEESECAKE FILLING
8 oz package cream cheese, room temperature
½ cup sugar
1 cup sour cream, room temperature
1 egg, room temperature
2 teaspoons matcha powder, completely dissolved in 2 tablespoons hot water
1 teaspoon vanilla extract
1 pint raspberry (garnish)

1. Preheat oven to 400°F. Line the bottom of a 7 x 3 inch springform pan with parchment paper.

2. Cream together butter and sugar in the bowl of an electric mixer. Scrape down the sides and add the flour. Mix until crumbly.

3. Press crumb mixture firmly into a lined 7 x 3 inch springform or push pan and refrigerate for 10 minutes. Bake in preheated oven for 15 minutes until the edge starts to brown.

4. Let the crust cool completely before adding cheesecake filling.

5. With an electric mixer on medium, beat cream cheese until smooth. With the mixer on, add sugar in a steady stream.

6. For the next few steps, only mix for 30 seconds and make sure to scrape down the side after the addition of each ingredient.

   • Add half the sour cream, mix for 30 seconds and scrape the sides of the bowl down. Repeat with remaining sour cream.
   • Add the egg.
   • Add the matcha and vanilla.

7. Pour the batter into the cooled crust. Tap pan on work surface to remove any air bubbles. Cover tightly with foil or with a silicone lid.

8. Place a trivet in the inner cooking pot and add 1 cup of water. Place the covered cheesecake on top of the trivet.

9. Close and lock the lid, making sure the steam knob is on Sealing/Locked. Pressure cook on high for 35 minutes.

10. Once the pressure cooking is done, natural pressure release for 10 minutes and then quick release the remaining pressure. The cheesecake should be mostly set, with only the center slightly jiggly.

11. Remove the pan and let it cool for an hour and refrigerate overnight or for at least 4 hours.

12. Run a knife along the edge of the cheesecake and transfer it onto a serving plate. Decorate and serve with raspberries.

Croissant Bread Pudding

Costco sells croissants by the dozen, so I always make sure that I save a few to make this bread pudding. The kids don't like the bourbon sauce but that's ok... More for the grown ups!

Makes 3-4 servings

3 stale croissants, ripped into 2 inch pieces
1¼ cups half and half
1 egg
2 egg yolks
½ cup sugar
¾ teaspoon vanilla extract

BOURBON SAUCE
2 tablespoons unsalted butter
¼ cup sugar
2 tablespoons whipping cream
1 tablespoons bourbon
pinch of salt

1. In a medium bowl, whisk half and half, egg, egg yolks, sugar and vanilla until well combined.

2. Place croissant pieces in a 7x3 inch deep baking pan that fits in your pressure cooker. Pour mixture over croissants. Gently press croissants down and let soak for 10 minutes. Cover with foil or silicone lid.

3. Place a trivet in the inner cooking pot and add 1 cup water. Place the pan on the trivet.

4. Close and lock the lid, making sure the steam knob is on Sealing/Locked. Pressure cook on high for 30 minutes.

5. Once the pressure cooking is done, natural pressure release for 15 minutes and then quick release the remaining pressure.

6. Carefully remove the dish from the pot. Let rest for 10 minutes.

7. Meanwhile, in a small saucepan, melt butter on medium heat. Whisk in sugar, whipping cream, bourbon and salt. Simmer for 3-5 minutes until thickened.

8. Serve warm bread pudding with bourbon sauce.

Lemon Curd

I love lemon anything! I don't think I would ever go back to making lemon curd on the stove top after making it in the Instant Pot. This is delicious on yogurt, cheesecake, ice cream, in sweet rolls, in cakes and tarts… I could go on and on and on…

Makes 2 cups

3 large eggs
¾ cup sugar
½ cup freshly squeezed lemon juice (3-4 lemons)
¼ cup unsalted butter, at room temperature
zest from 1-2 lemons
pinch of kosher salt

1. Put all ingredients into a blender or food processor and blend until well combined. Pour mixture into an oven-safe container that will fit in the Instant Pot.

2. Place a trivet in the inner cooking liner and add 1 cup of water. Place the container on top of the trivet and cover with a silicone lid or foil.

3. Close and lock the lid, making sure the steam knob is on Sealing/Locked. Pressure cook on high for 5 minutes.

4. Once the pressure cooking is done, natural pressure release for 10 minutes and then quick release the remaining pressure.

5. Remove the container. The lemon curd will still look curdled. Whisk until smooth.

6. Cool to room temperature before using.

Index